FOR THE BIRDS

The Life of Roger Tory Peterson

Peggy Thomas • *Illustrated by* Laura Jacques

CALKINS CREEK

Honesdale, Pennsylvania

For Francis
—PT

For Laurie and Sheri, with all my love
—LJ

Acknowledgments

I would like to thank the staff at the Roger Tory Peterson Institute of Natural History, Jamestown, New York, especially Marlene Mudge, special collections curator, who guided my research efforts and always knew what box to look in, and Mark Baldwin, director of education, for showing me a flicker up close. A special thanks to my editor, Carolyn P. Yoder, for asking the kinds of questions that can make a manuscript better. —PT

Deepest gratitude to the extraordinary and dedicated staff at the Roger Tory Peterson Institute, in particular Jim Berry, president; Mark Baldwin, who walked me through Jamestown in Roger's boyhood footsteps; Eugene Danielson and Sue Giomento of the Jamestown Community College Sheldon House for their warmth and hospitality; Don Hudson and the Chewonki Foundation; Karen Klotz Watras of ShellGirl Photography; Linda Westervelt for granting access to Roger's art studio in Old Lyme, Connecticut; the Connecticut Audubon Society and the director of EcoTravel, Andy Griswold, who gave me a glimpse of Roger's birding haunts; Elizabeth Gentile, Peterson Estate studio assistant, for generously donating her time and priceless insight; and all due thanks and praise to God for creating our wonderful world and the amazing creatures who share it. —LJ

The publisher thanks the Roger Tory Peterson Institute of Natural History and the Roger Tory Peterson Trust for the use of archival material and artwork for illustration purposes.

Permissions

Illustrations of bird silhouettes:
Adapted from *Peterson Field Guide to Birds of North America* by Roger Tory Peterson. Copyright © 2008 by Houghton Mifflin Company.

Page 29, illustration of *A Field Guide to the Birds*:
Adapted from *A Field Guide to the Birds*, written and illustrated by Roger Tory Peterson. Copyright © 1934 by Houghton Mifflin Company.

Text copyright © 2011 by Peggy Thomas
Illustrations copyright © 2011 by Laura Jacques
All rights reserved
For information about permission to reproduce selections from this book, please contact permissions@highlights.com.

Calkins Creek
An Imprint of Boyds Mills Press, Inc.
815 Church Street
Honesdale, Pennsylvania 18431
Printed in the United States of America

ISBN: 978-1-59078-764-9

Library of Congress Control Number: 2011920696

First edition
The text of this book is set in 14-point ITC Berkeley Oldstyle.
The illustrations are done in mixed mediums.

10 9 8 7 6 5 4 3 2 1

Some kids called him "Professor Nuts Peterson." He'd carry a snake in his pocket or a bird's egg in his cap. At eleven he was already in junior high school and yet refused to walk in line with the other kids. He looked as thin and gawky as a fledgling egret and sometimes smelled of skunk.

He didn't have lots of friends, preferring the company of the creatures in the woods near his home in Jamestown, New York. But the friends he did have were good ones, and they called him Roger. Roger Tory Peterson.

Roger loved being outdoors. His home at 16 Bowen Street was noisy, filled with his mother and father, sister and grandmother, and sometimes six cousins. From his woodland ramblings, Roger brought home abandoned nests and collected wildflowers that he carefully pressed between newspapers under the living-room carpet. He netted butterflies by day and moths by night.

But the city of Jamestown had a law. Children had to be off the street when the siren blew at 8:45 p.m. The first moths didn't come out until much later when the sky was black as ink and the streetlamps glowed. Roger didn't let a curfew stand in his way. He trotted to city hall and explained his problem. When he left an hour later, he held a piece of paper that read: "This permits Roger Peterson to catch moths around streetlights until 11 p.m." It was signed by the chief of police.

One fall, Roger pinned dozens of cocoons to his mother's lace curtains so they could wait out the cold. But in the middle of winter, when the coal stove blazed, the July-like heat inside brought the insects to life. The cases softened and new moths wriggled out. Green and yellow, brown and gold, they fluttered near lamps and laid sticky strands of eggs on the piano.

Sit-at-your-desk school wasn't much fun for Roger until a new teacher, Miss Hornbeck, formed a Junior Audubon Club, named after John James Audubon, who was America's first major wildlife artist. The club went on field trips, and for ten cents each student got a monthly leaflet describing a new bird.

On one hike up Swede Hill, Roger saw a clump of feathers sitting low in a tree. He watched it for several minutes, but it did not move. *It must be dead*, Roger thought. Silently he crept up to the brown bundle and reached out a finger. With one touch, it burst into life and flew out of sight. Roger's heart raced as fast as the startled flicker's. *So alive*, thought Roger. How wonderful to be free to fly anywhere. That was the moment Roger knew he would spend his life with birds.

When Roger wasn't bird-watching, he was usually reading a *Bird-Lore* magazine, his Junior Audubon leaflets, or his favorite book, *Two Little Savages* by Ernest Thompson Seton. The "savages" in the story were really two boys who spend a summer living off the land as the Indians did many years ago. Roger followed the instructions the main character, Yan, used to make a tipi, build a fire, or set a trap. But for Roger, the best part of the book was the page filled with birds.

In the story, Yan can't distinguish one kind of duck from another as they float far out on the lake. One day, Yan realizes that . . .

"All the Ducks are different; all have little blots and streaks that are their labels, or like the uniforms of soldiers. 'Now, if I can put their uniforms down on paper I'll know the Ducks as soon as I see them on a pond a long way off.'"

Yan draws each duck in its particular "uniform." He calls the drawings "far-sketches," and Roger never forgot them.

Roger loved to draw, too, and was delighted when Miss Hornbeck gave each student a box of watercolors and a color print by another famous bird artist, Louis Agassiz Fuertes. Roger got a blue jay. Carefully, he followed every line and matched each stroke. When he was done, Roger's blue jay was as handsome, strong, and joyful as the one he had copied. He knew then he wanted to be an artist.

Roger sketched chickadees, robins, and wrens in the margins of his schoolbooks. With each drawing he was remembering every bird's uniform.

It was difficult to paint birds from memory, and even harder to sit in the field and scribble the curve of the bill or the swoop of a wing before the feathered model flew off. Famous artists like Audubon and Fuertes painted from birds that were stuffed and mounted. Roger yearned to capture them in another way. He wanted a camera.

But a camera cost more than his father could afford on his salary from the furniture factory, so Roger took a job delivering the *Jamestown Morning Post*. At 3:30 every morning, Roger bundled his newspapers, then hoisted a sack of sunflower seeds. As he tramped through Jamestown, Roger filled more than twenty bird feeders that he set up along his paper route. By the time he got to school four hours later, he was ready for a nap. More than once, Roger fell asleep in class, his thatch of blond hair tousled on the desktop.

By the age of fourteen, Roger had enough money for his first camera, a Premo No. 9. Roger hauled the camera, tripod, and large glass negatives to the woods. Attaching a string to the shutter, he focused the lens on a bird at the feeder and hid. But sometimes Roger tripped over the string, scared the bird, and wound up with a picture of an empty feeder. That didn't stop Roger. He reloaded the camera, hid, and waited until he got just the right shot.

With his ears, Roger followed every chirp, whistle, and trill until he saw the bird that was singing. But even then, the bird was hard to identify as it flitted from branch to branch in the canopy of a tree or soared high against the bright sky. The only books about birds were thick and scholarly, written by scientists called ornithologists, who identified birds by shooting them first. It wasn't easy for Roger to read the descriptions and figure out if what he saw at a glance was a warbler or a finch. But Roger had eagle eyes and recorded everything he saw.

I saw the yellow head shine in the sun, and the white marks on each wing; I knew instantly that these were yellow headed blackbirds.

A noticeable thing about the goldeneyes was that they had stubbier heavier set bills than most other ducks.

Brown creepers have the habit of lighting at the base of the tree and climbing up.

Head — Seal Brown
Neck — " "
Light diffused spot behind the eye
IRIS — White (?)
Cere — Cream
Basal half of bill — dark
Front half of bill — Pinkish with
three white spots — the
first of which encircles
the top of the bill
Nass — black
Tail — dark
Wings and back — dark with
broad buffy margins on
the feathers — quite con-
trasty
Breast — Buffy with
darker vermiculations
Speculum(?) — White

Name	where seen	when seen	see
...ted blue warb.	in bush	May 6	May
Pheasant	on ground	May 7	May
	on ground	May 10	May
...len...	in...	May 10	May
...catcher	in...	May 11	May
...nian Warbler	in d...	May 11	May
...lia Warbler	in bush	May 11	May
...bird	in tree	May 12	June
...breasted Grosbeak	in tree	May 12	May
...crowned sparrow	in bush	May 12	May
...nut...ed Warbler	in bush	May 12	May
...om...	on spile	...y 13	May
Black...	...ing	...y 13	May
Ruby thr. Humming...		...15	May
Mourning Dove	fly...	M...6	M...
...t	in bush	May...	May 1...
		May...	May 1...

Birds seen in our block. (In the
heart of Jamestown.) including ones flying ove...
1. Goldfinch   18. Goose sp?
2. English sparrows   19. Yellow warbler
3. Downy woodpecker   20. Baltimore oriole
4. Junco   21. Chimney swift
5. Chickadee   22. B...
6. Tree Spar...

Each time Roger headed out the door with his field glasses or camera equipment, his father sighed. Why couldn't his son learn something useful, he wondered, like carpentry? How was he going to make a living drawing birds? He worried about Roger's future.

Roger worried about the birds. He kept track of when birds arrived in the spring and when they migrated in the fall.

April 3rd, 1924

Noticed a small bird perched on a twig, flirting its tail incessantly.
It was a Phoebe.
This is four days earlier than last year.

Everyone in high school knew what Roger was destined to become. When he graduated at sixteen, the caption beside his yearbook photo read: "Woods! Birds! Flowers! Here are the makings of a great naturalist."

Roger would have loved to study ornithology in college, but he could not afford it. Instead he took a job in Jamestown painting pagodas on black lacquer furniture. Roger's boss was impressed with his skill and encouraged him to display his work and go to art school.

At seventeen, Roger entered two bird paintings in a prestigious art show at a national birding convention in New York City. As soon as he heard that his paintings had been accepted, Roger began saving his money so that he could attend, too.

On a cool November day in 1925, Roger hurried to the American Museum of Natural History, where the convention was taking place. As he walked through the polished halls, Roger marveled at the wedge of geese suspended by invisible wires above his head, and gawked at the framed paintings by Audubon, Fuertes . . . and Peterson.

A noise startled Roger as he stared at his own name boldly scrawled in the corner of the canvas. Standing behind him was the great painter Louis Agassiz Fuertes, admiring Roger's work. The artist spoke of brushstrokes and highlights, but Roger was too stunned to remember many of his comments. Then Fuertes handed Roger a flat, red sable brush. "Take this. You will find it good for laying in background washes." Roger fingered it, noticing flecks of white paint in the heel of the bristles. Fuertes had used it, and Roger treasured the gift that made him feel like a real artist.

Roger enjoyed the freedom of being away from home. He was as determined as a woodpecker after a bug to save his money so he could move to New York City the following year and study at the Art Students League.

Leaving the nest meant new experiences, new friends, and new birds. Roger shared a family's small apartment in Brooklyn, New York, where the blast of barge whistles became as familiar as birdcalls. Each morning, Roger rose with the robins and took the subway to a job decorating furniture. In the afternoon, he raced to Manhattan to sketch models in art class. On weekends he went bird-watching.

Dear Mother,—
Went birding at Newark Bay
yesterday, a wonderful trip—
lots of birds—3 of which
I had never ever seen in my life
. . . weight on arrival—148 lbs
—weight now 146 lbs . . .
    all yours, Roger

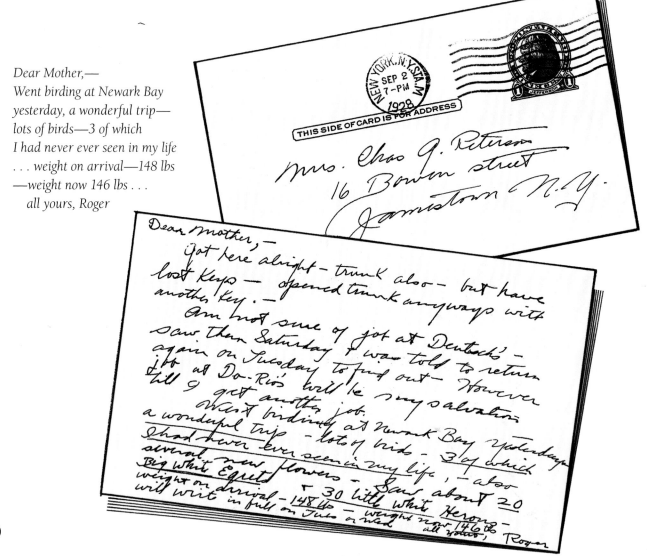

One day as he mucked through a marsh looking for rails, he parted the reeds and found another birder his age doing the same thing. It was Allan Cruickshank, a member of the Bronx County Bird Club. Although it sounded stuffy, the club was a group of nine young men who were just like Roger. They loved the thrill of the chase, listing as many birds as they could find. They made Roger the tenth member.

Sharing opera glasses and using pages torn from a bird book found in the trash, the club members sighted snowy owls masquerading as bundles of newspapers at the Hunts Point dump, scarlet tanagers downed by fog in Central Park, and a purple-breasted gallinule swimming in the Harlem Meer.

When school let out for summer, Roger worked as the nature counselor
at Camp Chewonki in Wiscasset, Maine. Like goslings, the campers
followed him on bird walks. One time, Roger became so focused on a
bird that he waded straight through a pond to get to it on the other side.
He was a natural teacher, and his enthusiasm was contagious. At the end
of the summer of 1931, the director of Chewonki invited Roger to teach
art and natural history at the Rivers School in Boston. That meant giving
up art school, but it also meant a salary with room and board. Jobs were
hard to find in the middle of the Great Depression, so Roger accepted.

Roger did not teach his bird-study class in the traditional way,
memorizing long Latin names or reading confusing descriptions. He
taught his students to identify birds the way he had learned—by their
uniforms, or field markings.

Since his technique of bird identification worked so well in his class,
perhaps it would work for anyone interested in birds. He was only twenty-
three years old and had never written a book before, but Roger set out to
create a new kind of bird book, one for people who knew nothing about
birds. A book he had wished he owned when he was a boy in Jamestown.

Roger knew that watching a bird in the field meant you had just a second or two to remember its shape, color, and size before it flew out of sight. So Roger painted only the memorable bits as Yan had done in his far-sketches. Simple outlines against a light background showed a bird's shape, and Roger added arrows to point out the most important field markings that distinguished one bird from another.

Like an owl, he worked at night in his cramped room, sketching and painting. On weekends he studied stuffed specimens at museums and spent hours in the field double-checking the descriptions of the nearly five hundred species he would include in the book.

Roger wasted no words. He wrote the same way as he had in his childhood journals. His descriptions were clear and as brief as an out-of-breath guide giving a snippet of information before jogging headlong into the brush. "The only *small* Owl with ear-tufts," he wrote about the screech owl. Roger emphasized what birders needed to know right there in that moment and fit it into a book small enough to put in a birder's pocket.

ADULT
BLACK-CROWNED
NIGHT HERON
IMMATURE
AMERICAN
BITTERN
LEAST
BITTERN
YELLOW-CROWNED
NIGHT HERON
ADULT
IMMATURE
LITTLE BLUE
HERON
GREAT BLUE
AMERICAN
EGRET
SNOWY
EGRET
HERONS

After three years of work, *A Field Guide to the Birds* was published. Roger was thrilled when he saw it in a bookstore window. But it was 1934. Millions were out of work, and a great many families lived in poverty. The book cost $2.75, as much as dinner for a family of four. Roger and his editor worried that it would not sell.

Perhaps everyone needed a diversion from the dismal times of the Depression. Perhaps people liked the idea of being as free as a bird as much as Roger did. Whatever the reason, Roger's field guide sold out within weeks.

Instantly, Roger, the gangly, self-made "nut" from Jamestown, was a famous naturalist. He wrote for *Bird-Lore* magazine, updated the Junior Audubon leaflets he loved as a child, and created another field guide for western birds. He visited schools, spoke to bird clubs, and promoted bird conservation.

All over the country, people began bird-watching and hanging bird feeders, their "Peterson guides" tucked into knapsacks or kept handy by the window. But as this peaceful hobby grew, the world was gearing up for war.

In 1943, Roger was drafted into the army. Wearing the plumage of a soldier, Roger moved with his wife, Barbara, to Washington, D.C., where he designed camouflage and illustrated military handbooks. But birds were always on his mind. One day, Roger found a prairie horned lark's nest on the drill field and convinced his captain to change the troop's parade route so the nest would not be disturbed.

Each night he painted bird portraits in the bathroom, because the best light was over the medicine cabinet.

Then the army sent Roger to Florida. For three months, he studied the effects a new pesticide had on birds. Although not much was known about the chemical DDT, Roger warned against its use. It killed insects, a vital food source for birds.

When the war ended, Roger felt that familiar sense of freedom and took flight. He hung over cliffs, submerged himself in swamps, and crouched under canvas to get just the right camera shot. He revised his first field guide and wrote another one for Europe.

By 1954, it was time to make a nest of his own. With his wife
and two sons, Roger settled into a house in Old Lyme, Connecticut,
surrounded by plenty of wilderness and an abundance of birds. It was
there in 1957 that Roger first noticed that something horrible was
happening.

"I scanned the marsh through my telescope. I saw the usual number
of adults about—but where were the young [ospreys]?"

No osprey eggs hatched that year. Throughout the Northeast,
peregrine falcons were also disappearing, and down South, bald eagle nests
were empty. Roger and other scientists believed that the cause might be the
widespread spraying of DDT, the pesticide he had studied years ago.
Someone had to stand up for the birds before they vanished completely.

Along with others, Roger spoke to birders and businessmen,
scientists and politicians.

Because he had sparked the world's appreciation for birds, people
listened. In 1972, the government banned the use of DDT in the
United States.

Roger did not stop there. He continued to speak for the birds
wherever they were in trouble. He migrated each year from his home
in Old Lyme to roost with birds all over the world—blue-footed
boobies in the Galápagos Islands, flamingos in Kenya, and penguins in
Antarctica—always returning to the nest to write and to paint.

On July 28, 1996, Roger worked in his studio. As focused as a heron after a fish, he perched on the edge of his seat. His thinning crest hung over his eyes as he painted a flycatcher he would never finish. That evening, at the age of eighty-seven, Roger died in his sleep. It would take a flock of friends to do the job that Roger had once done alone in a cramped room years ago—complete a new edition of *A Field Guide to the Birds*, the book that started it all.

Some people called him a naturalist, artist, photographer, teacher. But he was just Roger. Roger Tory Peterson. And he lived his life for the birds.

More About Roger Tory Peterson
August 28, 1908–July 28, 1996

Roger shared his passion for birds with three wives. He was married briefly to his first wife, Mildred. He and his second wife, Barbara, had two sons, Tory and Lee. Virginia, his third wife, worked closely with Roger and created the maps that appeared in the fourth edition of *A Field Guide to the Birds*.

Today, more than seven million copies of his field guide have been sold, and the "Peterson Identification System" is used in more than fifty Peterson Field Guides to identify everything from seashells to stars. His system was even adapted by the military to identify enemy planes in World War II.

Early in his career, Roger was the director of education for the National Audubon Society as well as art director of *Bird-Lore*. In addition to the field guides, he went on to write twenty-five other books and contributed to many more with his writing, editing, art, and photographs. He received twenty-two honorary degrees and hundreds of awards, including the Presidential Medal of Freedom, the highest honor for an American civilian. And as an artist, he is widely recognized as the wildlife painter who carried on the legacy of John James Audubon and Louis Agassiz Fuertes.

In 1993, the Roger Tory Peterson Institute of Natural History was built to carry on Roger's legacy as a teacher. Roger's passion to educate people and to protect birds was strong. He believed fervently what is etched on his headstone: "Birds cannot speak for themselves. I must speak for them," which is why he spent most of his life traveling in support of local conservation groups. Over his lifetime he saw nearly half of all the nine thousand known bird species in the world and traveled to every continent, including Antarctica to photograph his favorite birds, penguins.

The Peterson Effect

Before Roger wrote his field guide, women paraded around in feathered hats, and scientists believed you had to shoot a bird in order to identify it. Birds were just nameless creatures that were pests, decoration, or food.

But with the development of field glasses (binoculars), birders began to identify *living* birds. It took Roger many years to master bird identification, but his field guide allowed others to learn quickly. Soon people were calling birds by their right names. The field guide's subtitle, *A Bird Book on a New Plan*, signified just how revolutionary this idea was.

Once people learned the names of birds, they began to care about their survival, tracking migrations and recording populations. These delicate creatures, so sensitive to changes in their habitat, became an early warning of environmental problems. DDT, for example, accumulated in the bodies of animals, moving up the food chain in increasing concentrations. It caused raptors, at the top of the food chain, to lay brittle eggs that never hatched. When Roger noticed the decline in ospreys, he was wise enough to look for a reason and find a solution before more animals were harmed.

That wisdom is now passed along to you. Roger spent his whole life sharing his knowledge in the hope that you, too, will learn about the birds in your neighborhood and have the wisdom to protect the planet we all share.

The other creatures with which we share this world have their rights too, but not speaking our language, they have no voice, no vote; it is our moral duty to take care of them.

—RTP

Selected Bibliography

Books

Carlson, Douglas. *Roger Tory Peterson: A Biography*. Austin: University of Texas Press, 2007.

*Devlin, John C., and Grace Naismith. *The World of Roger Tory Peterson: An Authorized Biography*. New York: New York Times Books, 1977.

*Peterson, Roger Tory. *All Things Reconsidered: My Birding Adventures*. Edited by Bill Thompson III. Boston: Houghton Mifflin, 2006.

————. *Birds over America*. New York: Dodd, Mead, 1964.

*————. *A Field Guide to the Birds: A Bird Book on a New Plan*. Boston: Houghton Mifflin, 1934, 1967, and 1980 editions.

————. *How to Know the Birds: An Introduction to Bird Recognition*. 2nd ed. Boston: Houghton Mifflin, 1957.

————. *Wild America*. With James Fisher. Boston: Houghton Mifflin, 1955.

Rosenthal, Elizabeth J. *Birdwatcher: The Life of Roger Tory Peterson*. Guilford, CT: Lyons Press, 2008.

*Seton, Ernest Thompson. *Two Little Savages, Being the Adventures of Two Boys Who Lived as Indians and What They Learned*. Garden City, NY: Doubleday, 1959 edition. First published in 1903.

Articles

Kaufman, Kenn. "Gentle Giant." *Audubon*. July–August 2008.

Lager, Margaret Peterson. "Later Tales of the Early Bird." *Chemung Valley Audubon Society Bulletin*. May 1975.

————. "Tales of an Early Bird." *Chemung Valley Audubon Society Bulletin*. February 1975.

Peterson, Roger Tory. "Endangered Wildlife." Excerpts from keynote speech at Earthcare Conference at the United Nations, New York, June 6, 1975. (Reprinted from *The Conservationist Magazine*, December 1975.)

*————. "Evolution of a Field Guide." *Defenders of Wildlife*. October 1980. defenders.org.**

————. "My Top Ten Birds." *International Wildlife*. March–April 1996.

*————. "The Osprey: Endangered World Citizen." *National Geographic*. July 1996.

Websites**

Houghton Mifflin Harcourt. Official publisher's site for Roger Tory Peterson. houghtonmifflinbooks.com/peterson/rtp/biography.shtml

National Audubon Society. audubon.org

Roger Tory Peterson Institute of Natural History. rtpi.org

Take a Trip

To learn more about Roger, visit the Roger Tory Peterson Institute of Natural History at 311 Curtis Street, Jamestown, New York. Explore the same woods that young Roger did. Listen and look for birds on the guided trails that wind through wetlands to a pond. Inside, much of Roger's artwork is on display. Follow Roger's growth as an artist from the original field-guide drawings to his expert brushwork on life-sized bird portraits. Pick up a pair of binoculars sitting on any window ledge and watch the action at the bird feeders, check out the library, or participate in one of the many special events the institute sponsors.

*Source for quoted material in text. Additional quotations are taken from Peterson's personal papers housed at the Roger Tory Peterson Institute: Peterson's "Fourth Year Bird Study," 1923; untitled birding journal, 1924; Letter to Mother, 1928; and *The Red and Green*, Jamestown High School yearbook, 1925.

**Websites active at time of publication